ALSO BY JOHN ASHBERY

POETRY
Some Trees
The Tennis Court Oath
Rivers and Mountains
The Double Dream of Spring
Three Poems
The Vermont Notebook
Self-Portrait in a Convex Mirror
Houseboat Days
As We Know
Shadow Train
A Wave
Selected Poems
April Galleons
Flow Chart
Hotel Lautréamont
And the Stars Were Shining
Can You Hear, Bird

FICTION
A Nest of Ninnies
(with James Schuyler)

PLAYS
Three Plays

CRITICISM
Reported Sightings: Art Chronicles 1957–1987

WAKEFULNESS

WAKEFULNESS

POEMS BY

JOHN ASHBERY

FARRAR, STRAUS AND GIROUX · NEW YORK

Farrar, Straus and Giroux
19 Union Square West, New York 10003

Distributed in Canada by Douglas & McIntyre Ltd.
Printed in the United States of America
Designed by Jonathan D. Lippincott
First published by Farrar, Straus and Giroux in 1998
First paperback edition, 1999

Library of Congress Cataloging-in-Publication Data
Ashbery, John.
    Wakefulness: poems / by John Ashbery. — 1st ed.
        p.   cm.
    ISBN 0-374-52593-5 (pbk.)
    I. Title
PS3501.S475W26   1998
811′.54—dc21   97-45567

The author gratefully acknowledges the following
publications in which poems in *Wakefulness* first
appeared: *Boston Review, Conjunctions, Denver Quar-
terly, Grand Street, Jacket, London Review of Books,
The New Republic, The New Yorker, PN Review, Poetry,
Poetry Review, Salt, The Times Literary Supplement,*
and *Yale Review*

For Jim and Dara

CONTENTS

WAKEFULNESS

WAKEFULNESS

An immodest little white wine, some scattered seraphs,
recollections of the Fall—tell me,
has anyone made a spongier representation, chased
fewer demons out of the parking lot
where we all held hands?

Little by little the idea of the true way returned to me.
I was touched by your care,
reduced to fawning excuses.
Everything was spotless in the little house of our desire,
the clock ticked on and on, happy about
being apprenticed to eternity. A gavotte of dust-motes
came to replace my seeing. Everything was as though
it had happened long ago
in ancient peach-colored funny papers
wherein the law of true opposites was ordained
casually. Then the book opened by itself
and read to us: "You pack of liars,
of course tempted by the crossroads, but I like each
and every one of you with a peculiar sapphire intensity.
Look, here is where I failed at first.
The client leaves. History goes on and on,
rolling distractedly on these shores. Each day, dawn
condenses like a very large star, bakes no bread,
shoes the faithless. How convenient if it's a dream."

In the next sleeping car was madness.
An urgent languor installed itself
as far as the cabbage-hemmed horizons. And if I put a little
bit of myself in this time, stoppered the liquor that is our selves'
truant exchanges, brandished my intentions
for once? But only I get
something out of this memory.
A kindly gnome
of fear perched on my dashboard once, but we had all been instructed

to ignore the conditions of the chase. Here, it
seems to grow lighter with each passing century. No matter how you
    twist it,
life stays frozen in the headlights.
Funny, none of us heard the roar.

BALTIMORE

Two were alive. One came round the corner
clipclopping. Three were the saddest snow ever seen in Prairie City.

Take this, metamorphosis. And this. And this. And this.
If I'd needed your company,
I'd have curled up long before in the clock of weeds,
with only a skywriter to read by.
I'd have laved the preface
to the World's Collected Anthologies,
licked the henbane-flavored lozenge
and more. I'm presuming,
I know. And there are wide floodplains spotted with children,
investing everything in everything.
And I'm too shy to throw away.

PALINDROME OF EVENING

In other places where it was found
necessary for there to be buttons, expectations were naturally higher,
    and higher,
and higher.
Here,
a sow's purse translates into a silk ear, and communications
are jammed.
No one takes hold any more.
Look, the flower has escaped from its trellis,
the bear goes down into the lake.

In my second house rare footage
of metempsychosis plays endlessly, like a tune
variously tooted.
I often feel I'm a buyer,
but the painted carnival head reasons otherwise,
badgers me. There is no release in sight,
in the works, down the pike.
Horrified spectators jam the football field;
it was like night and day.
We can't go back to the restaurant;
the roof is snatched away.

What *were* expectations back then?
Do we know how high the astronauts carried us,
let us fall, bouncing for what seemed an eternity,
until all was well again?
I've got my cool
in these pants, keeping it for you.

COUSIN SARAH'S KNITTING

You keep asking me that four times.
Why trust me I think.
There is, in fact, nobody here.

Nobody in the past.
Nobody to turn to for advice.
A yellow flagpole rears thoughtfully.
Now if you were that nice.

He was pulled from space,
as from a shark. After they examined him
they let him go. What does that prove?

And called him Old Hickory.
As in hickory. No there were
at that time none living

out of a sideshow at the edge of a forest
and were mistreated in proportion,
with understanding, so they all grew

into the shade and for once it seemed
about right. Oh, call down to me.
It seemed about right.

Then there was something of a letdown.
Patrol boats converged
but it was decided that the . . .

and could continue its voyage
upriver
to the point where it tails off

and then there was a large misunderstanding.
It was misunderstanding, mudsliding
from the side where the thing was let in.

And it was all goose, let me tell you,
braised goose. From which a longing in the original
loins came forward to mark you.

So many brave skippers,
such a long time at sea. But I was going
to remind you of this new story

I can't remember, of the two chums meeting in the overfed waste land
    and it supported them. And one got
off at the front. The other wandered for days and daze, and by the time
    nobody remembered it it was summer again
and wandered around defensively. Sure the organ meat
was pumping and somebody's boy came up to the correct
thing at the well head. Sure as you can claim Dixie your tax accountant
wandered over the remaining riviera, all to be blue again. And the
    rascals . . .
and I was going to say keep it. You can keep it.
Granted she has no reputation, an eye
here, another clovered savior here, they pretend to us, and it was time
    for the firemobile too.

LAST NIGHT I DREAMED I WAS IN BUCHAREST

seeking to convince the supreme Jester
that I am indeed the man in those commercials.
Simultaneously it peaked in Bolivia, the moon,
I mean. Then we were walking over what seemed to be
heather, or was called that. The downtown riot
of free speech occurred. Plastered to its muzzle,
Randy the dog's decoding apparatus went astray.
By then it was afternoon in much of the world;
iced tea was served on vast terraces
overlooking a crumbling sea. You can't juggle
four toddlers. Three is enough. Out of the beckoning
sea they arrived, in white ruffles with black coin-dots
attached; the lawn was closer to a farm
this time; it mouthed "Farm." Will vacuumed the whole of space
as far as the mind-your-own-business wire stretched, that is,
from Cadiz to Enterprise, Alaska. We thought we had seen a few new
adjectives, but nobody was too sure. They might have been
gerunds, or bunches of breakfast . . .

ADDED POIGNANCY

What could I tell you? I couldn't tell you any other way.
We, meanwhile, have witnessed changes, and now change
floods in from every angle. Stop me if you've heard this one,
but if you haven't, just go about your business. I'll catch up with you
at the exit. Who are the Blands? The second change was perhaps
    nothing more than
the possibility of changes, one by one, side by side, until the whole
canyon was carpeted with them. Nice. Summer, it said,
ever rested my mind. Something occurs everywhere then,
an immediate engagement with the atmosphere
we'd like to have around, but it was big, then, and obvious,
and oh, this is for your pains. No, really. Take it. I insist.

He thought if he lived amid leaves
everything would surface again, by which he meant, balance out,
only look what this random memory's done to him!
He eats no more, neither does he sleep. A permanent bell tone
seems to create his hearing at each moment of his elevator. Obey. We're
in for it. There are no two ways about it. Wait—
did I say two ways? That's it! We'll fix his wagon with too many ways—
so it'll be lopsided, with no judges to pay, and we can all go home.
Sweetheart? I fancy you now—

Hence it ends up with a scenario of them all getting paid,
the bums, and walking out into the eternal twilight
with gurus and girlfriends on their arms, one for each fist.
I like that way about it. I'm making believe
it never happened, that we got this way
merely by having been here forever. Millions of languages
became extinct, and not because there was nothing left to say in them,
but because it was all said too well, with
nary a dewdrop on the moment of glottal expulsion.
But now I've got to go put out the signs on the chairs
so folks'll know when to stop, and where, really, only a poodle

separates us from this life and the next.
It will take us longer to get from here to there.
And the cigar band is ecstatic,
stunning in its mauve and gold obsolescence,
an erratic bloom on sheer night, faintly deleterious . . .

QUARRY

I was lying, lying down,
reading the last plays of Shakespeare.
A brat came to me, eyes squealing,
excitement its thing. Until I put two and two together

I never crossed the inlet
or realized what tributary meant.
O we all have fine times

in the spring she said.

No one needs to know pretty much
about that attitude I suppose,
yet there are riders, and puzzles, and soon,
baking at the long end of day
a poor cloud measures its shadow,
the intent of all those gone away.

LAUGHING GRAVY

The crisis has just passed.
Uh oh, here it comes again,
looking for someone to blame itself on, you, I . . .

All these people coming in . . .
The last time we necked
I noticed this lobe on your ear.
Please, tell me we may begin.

All the wolves in the wolf factory paused
at noon, for a moment of silence.

FROM SUCH COMMOTION

The dress code is casual, the atmosphere relaxed
in the licensed quarters of our city;
young couples graciously stopping beneath umbrellas
in the street . . .

And this is not a thing that matters:
walks on grass, through flaring Adirondack chairs.
You caught me napping said the belle-lettriste.

No, perhaps it's not that, that's the point. You've
been in to see these?
And we should have decided to go there, gone for a second time.
Yes, well, they're working on it, et cetera, etc.

The summer capital exits past us, we have to
sell product. It "fell through" the European system,
now it's time for avatars. At four in the morning
the art demonstrations begin, psalteries jingle, the whole damn ocean
is there, up for review, for us. It's just

that we don't understand. It's my negative capability acting up
again. Well, I'm within my rights.
It's like apples and pears, or oranges and lemons,
what I always say.

From nests as admirable as these, wallpaper islands,
the vivid flow reverses. That's in-house.
And we go as far
with them as possible, suffer stupid reverses, get plastered,

the goateed scorpion insists.
And it was while waiting for the drying to happen that we all got lost.
Please, he insisted, there's more to the point than two doors, O I know
it I said, I can't be damned to travel

any time. You should have pointed the way to me while I can,
while it's still light, otherwise what will all your gnashing accomplish,
the oatmeal? Please. Now just go away. It's
raining, the sun is shining, braver outdoors. Can we come listen to that.

MODERATELY

". . . and as the last will come a sort of moderato part, (which some is of multiple motions, quick, slow, hampered, expressive, popular, and peopled speech . . .)"

—*Stefan Wolpe*

The fox brooding and the old people smelling
and the tiebreaker—why did I not think of that?
Why have doubts upon me come? Why
this worldliness?
And I remember no longer at the age of sixteen,
and at the age of seventeen great rollers
eating into night, I uncared for,
stopping among the weeds along the way. Phantom
harvesters hovered. And the great, dry creekbed was a sea
of gravel and stones, the willows were capsized ships,
and none of it was for now.

There is a draught
in the room
and all along the room a sight that is like living
and looking out over a situation. The periods danced in a sentence,
and it was my way, the one I chose, even if I didn't choose it,
or like it; was all a coming on,
downpour,
marooned on slopes.

And then the burst of it.
He knew what the world's going to be like I think,
so why the explosions? And caught in the draught,
one fell from darkness, two fell from darkness,
yet another. Maybe that's dust a very fine kind of dust and I eat it,
it goes on thrumming, seated in the back row of the orchestra,
men masturbating here and there and like I said the clock
is tremendous,
wider than any minute hand or hour hand.

16

And sheepish it fell out of books:
the land of painful blisses,
the man who stubbed his toe.
All around us pain came sledding in,
and am I like this today, tomorrow, and two
tickets please, the boy and the ruffian come undone,
he was in the park, it was the salutary last person
to hoodwink you and all is well.

There were times a kind of cream was on the jagged borders
or suchlike events and carnivals, and you sat, smiling,
the tongue unleashed from its surroundings. Why was I never here?
Why such playacting? Didn't I ever realize the kernels *are* deep-seated,
that everyman will overrun his banks just like an errant stream,
and cardboard principles be jostled? O who
mentioned this session? What is the matter with truth and paying
and all over the paisley fields dominoes are braying,
a matter of luck, or chance, it seems? Who broke the next dish?

Why is that man crying,
what does he mean to do? Impertinent, in person,
what does he mean to do,
if these capers are not unusual
and bricks merge with sand, the unusual
at its best as usual, and can't we give up? What
would be the point of continuing? I can't smoke this weed,
I give it back, we are all blessed, commensurates within
a star where many things fit, too many, or not too many, whatever
it says about you, whatever saves.

ALIVE AT EVERY PASSAGE

Roll up your sleeves,
                       another day has ended. I am not a part of the vine
that was going to put me through school
but instead got sidetracked and wandered over the brink of an abyss
while we were having a good time
in full view of the nearest mountains. *Mon trésor,* she said, this is
     where I
disappear for a few moments, I want you to be brave.
Sure, nothing like a date in bed,
waking after midnight to the blank TV screen
that wants us all to listen to its cute life and someday understand
what rhomboids the earth took
on its way down to get us,
that we must be happy and sad forever after. No I don't think
it was in your best interests nor do I shave with an old-fashioned
     straight-edge,
you dolt. But I was coming to that,
doing the mystifying. So if he says not to be aloha, not again,
well gee in this old-fashioned bar, however will the runts learn from
     their again imploded
hair balls how straight everything is.

The rest, as they say, as they say, is history:
I captured a barracuda, it was midnight in the old steeple, the clans
     casually
moved on us, leggings barely jerked out of the ditch. It was folly
to be noticed, then, astir on the perhaps more urgent
surface of what becomes one, indeed comes to become one
through impossible rain and the sly glee of mirrored xylophones.
Say only it was one for the books,
and we, we did belong, though not to anything anybody'd recognize
as civil, or even territory. I need to subscribe,
now, history will carry me along and as gently leave me
here, in the cave, the enormous well-being
of which we may not speak.

THE BURDEN OF THE PARK

Each is truly a unique piece,
you said, or, perhaps, each
is a truly unique piece.
I sniff the difference.
It's like dust in an old house,
or the water thereof. Then you come
to an exciting part.
The bandit affianced
to the blind man's daughter. The mangel-wurzels
that come out of every door, salute the traveler
and are gone. Or the more melting pace of strolling players,
each with a collapsed sweetie on his arm, each
tidy as one's idea of everything under the sun is tidy.
And the wolverines
return, with their coach, and night,
the black bat night, is blacker than any bat.

Just so you know, this is the falling-off place,
for the water, where damsels stroll and uncles
know a good thing when they see one.
The park is all over.
It isn't a knee injury, or a postage stamp on Mars.
It is all of the above, and some other things too:
a nameless morning in May fielded by taut observers.
An inner tube on a couch.

Then we floated down the Great Array river, each
in our inner tube, each one a different color:
Mine was lime green, yours was pistachio.
And the current murmured to us mind your back
for another day. Are
you so sure we haven't passed the goalposts yet? Won't
you reconsider? Remount me to my source? Egad,
Trixie, the water can speak! Like a boy
it speaks, and I'm not so sure how little all this is,

how much fuss shouldn't be made about it. When another boy comes
to the edge of the falls, and calls, for it is late,
won't we be sorry for not having invented this one,
letting him fall by the wayside? Then, sure enough, waves
of heather recuse the bearers of false witness, they fly like ribbons
on the stiff breeze, telling of us: We once made
some mistake, it seems, and now we are to be judged, except
it isn't so bad, someone tells me you'll be let off the hook,
we will all be able to go home, sojourn and smile again, be racked
with insidious giggles like guilt. Meantime, jugglers swarm over the
    volcano's
stiff sides. We believe it to be Land's End, that it's
six o'clock, and the razor fish have gone home.

Once, on Mannahatta's bleak shore,
I trolled for spunkfish, but caught naught, nothing save
a rubber plunger or two. It was awful,
at that time. Now everything is cheerful.
I wonder, does it make a difference?
Are sailors waving
from the deck of their distraught ship? We aren't
envious though, life being so full of
so many little commotions, it's up to
whoever to grab his (or hers). The violin slices life up
into manageable hunks, and the fiddler knows not
who he is moving, or cares why people should be moved;
his mind is on the end, the extraordinary onus of finishing
what's set out for him. Do you imagine him better off than you?
My feet were numb, I ask him only, how do you carry this from here to
    over there?
Is there a flat barge? How many feet does a centipede have?
(Answer in tomorrow's edition.) I heard the weeping cranes,
telling how time was running out. It was Belgian,
they thought. Nobody burns the midnight oil for *this*,
yet I think I shall be a scholar someday, all the same.

The hours suit me. And the rubber corsages the girls wear
in and out of class. Sure, I'll turn out to be a nerd, and have to sit
in the corner, but that's part of the exciting adventure. I know things
are different and the same. Now if only I could tell you . . .

The period of my rest is ended.
I shall negotiate the fall, then go crying
back to you all. In those years peace came and went, our father's car
    changed
with the seasons, all around us was fighting and the excitement of
    spring.
Now, funnily enough, it's over. I shan't mind the vacant premise
that vexed me once. I know it's all too true. And the hooligan
ogles a calla lily: Maybe only the fingertips are exciting,
it thinks, disposing of another bushelful of ripe nostalgia.
Maybe it's too late,
maybe they came today.

AT THE STATION

Renewed by everything, I thought
I was a ghost. All we've got in the back seat are doors.

I was just thinking
it was time to go back, pick up the pieces,
place them on a stand. You are nearer
to the high-school orchestra.
Youth plays absorbed.
If it had its own way, we'd be
outside. The decision is HERE!

Already they're taking it down,
distributing the various parts to places built in the ground
just for them. Next, we'd be tiptoeing
up and down the station platform. Look,
I've brought you a box of candied chestnuts, for the great voyage
into the technical dream you will learn to read.
For us, it is enough that the grass grows
sideways into the loam,
and that the wind is curious, silent tonight.

ANOTHER KIND OF AFTERNOON

Remotely the unnamed keeps up with me.
It must be quite a time
since the last dignitaries visited with you.
Yes, and I'm about out of breath

for all the quiet cells we kept company in.
Must be a zillion years—
Look, here comes one of them.
I know I just met the czar's brother

in a book report. Soon it was time to return home,
past the midpoint, skipping-place.
Fierce, how that cloud suffocates
the sun, then is gracious for a while

but we can't go back there
due to the clamor, it's just as well
that they roll about
on the grass, young ones, old ones, the deer,

the pointer. And when you've imbibed as much
of the hurt as likes you, it's time for tag,
game that rolls down through our lives
over and over. You get what you have

to ask for, which turns out to be enough
to divide with the haphazard, rather ragged
assembly.
             We didn't go near the
windmill again for years, it was as though it had crumbled

in the imagination. Pretty soon six-pointed
purple stars stabbed us awake, and my goodness . . .

TANGLED STAR

A cup drips air,
peanuts fester. A wallaby streaks for the light,
suspenders down, indeed his pantleg is falling.
A ghost train appears over the snow-shrouded moor,
shoving us into silence. I decline the irregular verbs
of which our life is composed, but I cannot sing.
It stirs in the pencil box.
The ruler is too close for that.
Wind chimes grate against the door,
as though we never had one. Electricity
is named for the first time.

There are tensions. I suggest we try them out,
but the New England steeple looks sourly at us,
all coffins to the wind.

Alas, we are forbidden to worship the tensions,
even to play with them. If the next moon provides the addition,
the hearse its hamper of ham sandwiches, why then we will go,
as I told you we must. We are forever outdoors,
saving people's lives. The cattails get to see so much of us
that their contempt breeds civility, and the swamp
comes to seem right. Why hadn't it seemed so all along?
Now that it has gophers to chew on
we can imagine a less festive, more brackish
raison d'être of it. But we like it that our play be long,
and too many overseers crowd the hutch.
It is definitely time to move on.

Yet I had thought all of this was a party.
It is, but only in its duration, that sweeps us
down the stairs and over the side of a hill
where baubles float, and you get to interrogate that special someone.
In a flash, more finches, blue jays and fronds appear,
bronzed with a special effect of light, that says

it only to outdoors. To imagine what lies outside it
you would have to be a king or confidence man. And alas,
we have other plans for you. You are to come to see us
this evening, in the confusion of evening, to test our reflexes,
to speak to the dressmaker's dummy, and derive of it what comfort you
    can.
Your horoscope says so. What sign are you? Aw, Libra
with Pisces rising. Then I command you back to the cold

that you like so much, even though I had second thoughts
about it and everything. Can't you see the bear's paw
prints? They are elusively alive, held up by the trainer's
hoop, to be an example
to the ferocious wilderness. Here, take these herbs.

So many things, so many role models.
Their eagerness dances in the firelight.
We can't just say no to them, they have to live us
too. And in places where the water has ebbed the sky is midnight blue,
like ink spreading from a nib. They're all here, the catchers,
umpires, men in blue flannel suits, women
with a trace of tears like re-embroidered lace,
dusty with diamonds, seams in place. There is the mother;
she calls to the son. The tortoise and the hare
have come to tolerate us. Out on the lagoon
macaws are coughing. It is important to respect our situation.
One of them tries to get back to "normal,"
but the place is too exaggerated. Madame Nola is here.
And the bishop's children. And silly Irmgard.
And Rodney's commando. The teacher's pet. The cigar baron.
Marshal Tito. The young Eleanor Roosevelt.

DEEPLY INCISED

If this is July, why does it look like August?
Sadly growing up into the real world
I don't even ask these questions *myself*.
Why are the shutters drawn
over that restaurant?
The moon's backwash is like a deeply incised
hairnet against the stadium.
Bats drool into the gutter.

If everybody is so intent on illustrating what they *know*,
why is the ant syllabus closed?

TROPICAL SEX

Yes, making a point of using it
makes a point, and otherwise all is but fish scales
and fish delivery—the clear-eyed blue trough of song
in whose pit I stumbled. O Lord,
help me to get over it. That's better, for a minute
there I thought I was a goner
and now I brushed up this interesting world
of lutanists and lunacy, and afterlife
not unlike the one we were used to—
Gosh, it's so thrilling,
everyone is so nice,
one had almost forgotten chiggers existed,
and bedpans, and dumb ugly coffers
like the one we lived in.
But that is only a sign now.

Be warned. A slight distance.

Or picture an insect struggling.
But it's going to be all right, I tell you.
We can live in The Heights and conjecture interestingly
about how life is made, how a man is.paid
after all the contracts and ledgers are signed, blotted
in the sun. And surely one can stagger then,
get up and stagger to the nearest public telephone
and make slurping sounds at an invisible opponent: gone, warned
away, washed away. This siding came in with a crumpled
building already on it. Now only frogs can compute
the earth-sign that led gradually to dementia and panic.
The storage place is over there. I can see thistles
out of the corners of my eyes. It must be we are waiting

on another's aggression, handmaidens to the very plot
that would destroy us. We can
manage a giggle or handshake, but in the end the ink seeps through

and the person who did this wants very much to believe it,
has put himself inside us for this purpose. O chilblains,
weather vanes in the aching March wind,
did you want this ending? For this to happen
even as we were sitting all nice inside
the house, and by its hearth, and the brutal call
of the scarecrow fell like a hush over everything?
My friend thinks so—tell *her*
the bad news: "up to our ears in debt," playing a little
on the tidal lawn, abashed by our failure
to keep track of the consequences as they happened, and now a little
girl goes out to the squirrel. Hey, kid,
can I see your—
              Sorry, time's up.
We get to place a small white stone here at the crossroads;
it can be any one you like. Remember to vote. The clothesline has fallen
to the enemy somewhere. Yet the awnings are still prim and
      conspiratorial.
My chapter met and discussed you. Any number can play, the fleet's in,
and with the recyclables, our starched T-shirt.

THE FRIEND AT MIDNIGHT

Keeping in mind that all things break,
the valedictorian urged his future plans on us:
Don't give up. It's too soon. Things break. Yes, they fail
or they are anchored up ahead, but no one can see that far.
As he was speaking, the sun set. The grove grew silent. There
are more of us taking ourselves seriously now than ever,
one thought. We may never realize about our lives
till it's too late, and a man with a dog comes to shoot us.
I like to think though that everything is its own reward,
that liars such as we were made to last forever,
and each morning has a special chime of its own.

Thus we were pitted against the friend who came at midnight
and wanted to replace us with a song. We resisted furiously:
There was too much food on his table, the night was too black,
while all around us shrinking bands of outsiders
entered into negotiations with his darkness. It
seems to omit us, his reasoning, or in the well of time
we may be overdrawn, and cosmetics come to put a good face on us,
asking, why this magic wind, so many angles
against the river's prism and the burnt blue sky?
To which one answers, nothing is adrift
for long. Perhaps we will be overtaken
even in our happiness, and waves of passion drown us.
Now, wasn't that easy? A moment's breath and everyone
has gone inside to ponder the matter further.
Outside, children toboggan endlessly.

STUNG BY SOMETHING

but my advice is—be comfortable.
Wear a smock, with fractals. Be native!
You'll find people are more interested in your story,
and they will, too. Revisit

the recurrent tragedy of life.
Make sure it has its priorities straight.
Then—ziff! Jump off the end of a dock.
Color a monsoon yours, to do business and pleasure with.

With Smokey, everywhere seemed like pastime.
Girls in their girdles wandered up
amazed—they had never seen so many cheekbones.
The irises on the dump bloomed surlier that year—

too many tin cans. But you and I were deriding
ourselves, therefore it couldn't be over yet
and the past never happened here. Pounding
on his front door, one day or other,

the jasper eggs somehow knew my name.
It was all over, in fits. The tree-house
curtains were drawn, laughter strangely spattered the mist,
stippled the tenement wiring. Oh it's been gone

too long, tragedy again visits the dying shires,
tells one to hang in, it's over the top
with you. *Looks like
we've been invited to a party.* Treason peppered

the masts of my little skiff. Help! And then
an eternity of silence. Bores
shifted on the upper floors, there are not
enough spider-crabs, spiders of the sea,

for this embroidered doormat to clinch the departure bell.
Surely all's well—
we'd have heard about it otherwise. Strangers tell
this in shifts, for a little pleasure, a brittle hour.

THE LAST ROMANTIC

Not to stumble, to get to tell you something simple
about the way the grass was being waves, how we broke
the world after we made it. Then it was a thorn-bearing crescent.
Now you must be funny. Paranoid gigolos and candy,
lots of it, over the airways, in fact how could you,
you knew he was coming today. Well, better to squash
it once and for all. I was a fool for coconuts, I said
coconuts. Nobody believes me anymore, they think I've been
let out, but I haven't, I'm still locked up, and lovelorn.
Pretty please promise me a dish of scrolls.
After that one nip everything will be nasty and then it will be romantic.

They pass him with muffin heads down along the winter beach.
So many characters. They told him there were too many characters
in your novel, that the plot was still complicated, but still
they keep coming on, there must have been a leak, wait, it's not even
    that,
there are just too many people out there. Well I suppose it seems
so to you, who are not normal, but if you could see
it all from the outside you'd find how many are glued
to your coattails, and not too many, never less than enough,
and that includes children. My stars well I
never counted on all this being here. No, and neither
did your daddy, and it's quiet in the city,
too quiet, except for the largest vans and convertibles, and these
are safely filed under "European"—we can let everything go, really,
and then come back and look at it and pick it up.

Well it sure was farther the way
you always insist on taking us, me and one other person, but in
fine it was not a great distance, only a matter of some blocks
in one ward of the city. Say, I had a great
idea and now it's gone off and become useless.
So may I someday, sitting at play in my little unknown courtyard.

So may we all, while cats whine and grapes mature
and a prickly dust of unknown origin seems to rise upward from the
   seats.

SHADOWS IN THE STREET

She bit the bridge. A photograph can stomach it. I'll be in
some time in the middle of July. Now the best time
of the year is around now, none can gainsay August
and Mr. Random's tooth running in the street, he liked to say hi, it was
    just
him running, which is a bit awkward. A diagonal lipstick
chased him across the street. From there on in it was just damn
    melancholy,
no anchovies, nothing in particular, nothing to say. If so why, why do it,
says Peter, who fought hard for the post, fought it and won,
and why we are here, in the middle of a secondary terrain, mad and
    absorbed
by life, by the truth, as always.

But the nice part
I was going to say is fenced out. Take to the hills then. There goes
one petal, the tree is falling apart, zounds I can do almost nothing
while the hills come and separate us, plant us in tomorrow
or until the last dish is unearthed.

Out crept a third one.
Savannas that have been dangerous, now no one remembered,
the evil shifting of feet denounced the lady travelling salesman
to our liposuction expert. A single afternoon cooking at the stove
and all is more or less gone over, too bad
the futile Molotov cocktail exploded
but in any case in another land, with more furniture than we expected.
So we said, grant us this, it shall be done in another kingdom
as in the king's den. Don't let the roof fall in!
I was kind of sidelined by the barber pole
but explained practically about the dark petal, that it was good
and we were appearing in its time, and shall be heaven, about time,
    about
that point. Rockets lifted. Read me. There is no point to all this listless
hive. He took off in a manner that betokened bats

when it was over and they came over. It's time, now, some are good and
     alone,
lost up unto the rest. They can go and cancel
around it's too moot to be played at. They are, for the rest unsavory,
thyme in the corral, three jumps from last school
the patio ignited, sworn to safe-conduct, like bread out of a school
conducted at last to here.

THE EARTH-TONE MADONNA

What were you telling him about,
and why were veins implanted in the marsh
where everyone looks? Today
is the first day of spring, I think.
Sailing near us on a monocle,
the spray tapped and jiggled,
forever like a lifeboat.

And true some were found perjured
in cornshocks, there was no meat left that day,
no edge one could run around on.
There were peepers in the loose chaos called
oblivion, and not much else on the table.
Miss—er—Jones, what is the order of events?
I think not sir she cabled
from a vantage point in Toronto where all ships
and trains have their terminus. And if it's Wednesday?
Then man the egrets, the snowplow is coming
to rest where all of us have our workshoes on
and it will be a tough call to divide up the rope
and Saturday.

There was no hope in the statue
of the saint, eyeballs collapsed, sloping forward
like a scythe, and yet we came to know
how he was doing, and appreciated a chat
at his knees. Now this was only the fourth time
any had done so. So we squeegeed
the happy-face off home plate, and bunches
of aristocrats all around us applauded
what came to seem fair, and in time
were whisked away—the ox in his pumps,
forgotten for daydreaming, the tangled marl
of old Sol's beard. Everything was decimated,
which was devastating, yet we went on

living, along the row we had been set down in
and soon we had reached the end. A conniving quiver
set compass needles skittering, prize lists
fairly glittering. And I looked to thee
to see what a retroactive spouse might be
yet we got lost somehow in the confusion
attendant on the formal victory. We were back
home, in fact, but no one thought to look
for us there. We were let out to pasture
in the shade, and six more volumes dovetailed.
The first part of the novel was now complete,
a hundred years in the making, yet its style
seemed chaste, if not downright lackluster, in the best sense,
as many terriers were starting to run,

yappingly. If there was a space for us
in all this fireside, it got debunked. We were kept waiting
right up until the announced departure,
and so became part of humanity. Part and parcel, I was going to say.

In the dim
eclectic din, beaters waited.
Let's handsel it, love, O my love, I said.

DEAR SIR OR MADAM

After only a week of taking your pills
I confess I am seized with a boundless energy:
My plate fills up even as I scarf vegetable fragments
from the lucent blue around us. My firmament,

as I see it, was never this impartial.
The body's discomfiture, bodies of moonlit beggars,
sex in all its strangeness: Everything conspires
to hide the mess of inner living, raze
the skyscraper of inching desire.

Kill the grandchildren, leave a trail
of paper over the long interesting paths in the wood.
Transgress. In a word, be other than yourself
in turning into your love-soaked opposite. Plant
his parterre with antlers, burping
statue of when-was-the-last-time-you-saw Eros;

go get a job in the monument industry.

THE LAUGHTER OF DEAD MEN

Candid jeremiads drizzle from his lips,
the store looks as if it isn't locked today.
A gauzy syllabus happens, smoke is stencilled
on the moss-green highway.

This is what we invented the suburbs for,
so we could look back at the lovable dishonest city,
tears clogging our arteries.

The nausea and pain we released to float in the sky.
The dead men are summoning our smiles and indifference.
We climb the brilliant ladder toward their appetites,
homophobes, hermaphrodites, clinging together like socks
hanging out to dry on a glaring day in winter.

You could have told me all about that
but of course preferred not to,
so fearful of the first-person singular
and all the singular adventures it implies.

DISCORDANT DATA
for Mark Ford

Still in spring, my coat
travels with the pack, unbuttoned as they.

The weather report is useless. So,
sigh and begin again the letter.

"This is the first time in weeks
I've had to communicate with you. It all

falls, in balls of fire. I guess the
North Dakota landscape doesn't do much for you. Have you

no conscience, or conscious, conscious conscience?
May I remind you that every sentence, everywhere,

ends with a period? A disclaimer of sorts?"
He thought we'd gotten to the middle of the grass.

His glass fire hydrants can have no end.
Oh it was just an idea;

there, don't rail. The posse is coming
by for drinks, we can skip enslavement today.

Concentrate, instead, on this day's canonicity.
It has to be from somewhere,

right? Many prisoners have left downtown, the old man
assents. He was tremendous and bald. Liked a practical joke

now and again. Look, the white rain is writing on the wall
of his saloon. Could be he was over the hill,

we'd assumed, but the flapping in the net's too
strong for that. Don't you agree? Have you

had any further ideas on the subject? Yes, you
could well afford to give up a few.

BOGUS INSPECTIONS

The things that were in the drawer were dispersed a long time ago.
Some were wetted by snow. Others were dry but could not refract the
    light.
On the harbor's side a frazzled touch obtained.
Peace of mind fell through a grating in the sidewalk
where it lay visible for a few hours

and then it went away. Anyway, what can I tell you?
Not the things you want to hear, I suppose.
Nor can your interest deflect my moodiness. I shovel all the things you
    want to hear
into a wheelbarrow and leave it on your front step.
Perhaps some of it will reflect on me, on you, hell,
who knows what will jump out of it?
Some other passports were issued. Pilgrims
with scrip and staffs lined the stairwell and the near reaches of the
    street
in the moony swell that always seems to take over there, at a certain
    point
when I'm far from you. That's the message of it all—
of life, even.

You say you shied away from every event
in our small house. Yet at the end it turned sociable;
there was a breeze in the flags that they noticed
and one felt like running toward some inescapable doom, just for the fun
    of it.

Some were on vacation, a busman's holiday
they called it, and would have it no other way. Gradually my hands
    readjusted
to the stitchery in the tablecloth. If it was going to be *this* way, why
not pass the wine around again. Hoist up your stocking
to where the emerald stickpin has pierced it, a joy
for all to see. Say, I suddenly realized I want

to be you along for the ride. Why not? And the breeze
is cool.

You see, in your pharmacopeia of battered notions
just the right things prevail. A man is his house. Two naked girls
are in tubetops. Fun to see. A lazy susan spins round again:
What has it brought you this time?
Are there going to be summer suckers?
What'll be the big surprise?

Good news. The universe has been challenged again
by a schoolboy in South Orange. And oh yes,
long division has come out on top.

To see you the way you go this way
is to know the marvelous state of tulips in this our parkway.
What goes around comes around. The medicine dropper approached the
    sky.
This will soon cure *that*.
So wonderful you could see us again.

FLOATINGLY

Kill the white beaches, the hotel, bugs!
The crumbs on a table sang this song to insulate themselves,
but the chickens merely pecked harder. We do, we don't, we do, we do
    mean
to vacuum these crumbs, unless someday an idiot boy
pass through the wood on his way to the ballpark,
tossing his cap unassumingly, for what is, in fact, a gesture?
It is only a gesture. So, sure, morons
can be on your side of the spleen fence: It's only gurus
matter to outsiders, after all, the lame girl said.

She spoke, and I averred:
No one who has known this beach can undo the righteousness that begat
    it
out of sand, close to a fence.
By the same token, one needs two tin cans.

And let the browsers beware, she famously
ad-libbed, for chickens are like jurists in at least one sense:
Neither is wanted when the old line undulates,
shrieking its core across water.

No saffron impediment to evening's fine-sanded
elliptical body,

for the presence of a mote is always singular.
Towheaded ideas learn from and are transformed by them.
We have only too much lettuce, lettuce to give away.
Our fronds shall not know us
nor apocryphal lectures train us to eye the side aisles.

TENEBRAE

For a little snow you get your asking price:
the Ace of Wounds, star of tubs, brushfires
from there to here like an afterthought,

and this suddenly not all that you willed it to be.
We marched in different directions.
Once a week there's a very big field day.

Plant two skyscrapers. Then the moat will be less
unexpected. It's coming round to you again;
indeed, it dances. And in this starting to be something

something disappears, but a shine prevails.
And they don't pay attention,
and they don't pay attention, that's all I can say.

See what the prisoners of war are all about.
How close are you? Rocks seep into the night
and the clay gets the attention it deserves.

We build and build our shadow-pulpit,
then seize morning when it comes,
in chirrupy stride: names of the lost ships,

lasting until today, until nostalgia sets in. We're home
in what passes for a city in America (are the streets

laughing at us?). We can't drive yet,
or even walk.
And one is given the run of the land.

Outside my window the Japanese driving range
shivers in its mesh veils, skinny bride
of soon-to-be-spring, ravenous, rapturous. Why is it here?
A puzzle. And what was it doing before, then? An earlier
puzzle. I like how it wraps itself
in not-quite wind—
                  sure enough,
the time is up. What else do you have in your hand?
Open your hand, please. My elder seraph
just woke up, is banging the coffee-pot lid
into place. See! the coffee flows
crazily to its nest, the doldrums are awake,
jumping up and down on tiptoe, night-blindness ended.

And from where *you* stand,
how many possible equations does it spell out?

My hair's just snoring back.
The coprophagic earth yields another of its
minute reasons, turns to a quivering mush,
recovers, staggers to its feet, touches the sky
with its yardstick, walks back to the place of received,
enthusiastic entities. Another year . . . And if we had known last spring
what the buildings knew then, what defeat, it would have turned to mud
all the same in us, waved us down the escalator,
past the counter with free samples of fudge, to where the hostess stands.
This was never my idea, shards, she says. This
is where the anonymous donors carved their initials in my book,
to be a puzzle for jaycees to come, as a nesting-ground
is to an island. Oh, we'd waddle
often, there, stepping in and out of the boat
as though nobody knew what time it was, or cared
which lid the horizon was. We'd get to know
each other in time, and till then it was all a camp meeting, hail-
fellow-well-met, and the barstools

reflected the ceiling's gummy polish, to the starboard
where purple kings sit, and it was too late for today,
the newspapers had already been printed, telling their tale
along avenues, husks of driftwood
washed ashore again and again, speechless, spun out of control.
What a gorgeous sunset, cigarette case, how tellingly
the coiled rope is modelled, what perfume
in that sound of thunder, invisible! And you wonder
why I came back? Perhaps *this* will refresh your memory,
skateboard, roller skates, the binomial theorem picked out in
brutish, swabbed gasps. All the way to the escape clause
he kept insisting he'd done nothing wrong, and then—pouf!—it was
curtains for him and us, excepting these splinters
of our perpetual remainder, reminder
of all those days to come, and those others, so far back
in the mothering past.

ANY OTHER TIME

A couple of shivers of attitude
ago the ship coasted out of sight
to its life in rain.

More morbid mongrels munching
and the news from over there clouds
the hockey pageant's desperate coda,
that shakes with the glitter of edges, of the steep
vocabulary that's coming . . .

All around us fires
are trained at the center, neatest thing
that ever happened. I'll bye-bye you
in blue
if it's the last thing we do.

So we say: Someone had an urge, a whim,
and lightning began there. On all
roads we merely trespass, finding a level,
store-bought thing. Like buying a grapefruit
and having it displayed. Yes and we have teas,
boots for the sore, beds for the weary,
a whole warehouse full of notions,

and this. Makes you kinda comfy.
The less said the more we'll shut up about it—
on the cusp, actually.

PROBABLY BASED ON A DREAM

Like you've done it before—
Are you working hard? Hello? Mrs. Grizzli?
                    Only the happy few know what keeps us
from ballooning into our strength. And when we try
                    to capture wisps from the rocket,
sinking in the hay, there are those who tell you
                    to come again another day,
that the past is soiled and forgotten. Yet neither
                    you nor I know what happens in the thud
of cannon threatening to take off with the wild ducks
                    thunderously, and you, if I'm not
mistaken, were around here once, once too often
                    the landlady tells me. Quick! Where is
your whoop? How unexpectedly have we arrived? In a brusque mountain
                    workshop where tankas are forged, and the truth comes
unsliced, like bread, the captains and the pageants err and repeat;
                    for nothing all along was it?
But someday, I know, my idol will slip me a pill
                    for as long as bunkers repeat themselves. Alyssa?

Shovel the maps into the diving helmet.
The press cuttings have come to grief;
wind slaps the high buildings.
You too know Kokomo, O unpreceded one.

THE VILLAGE OF SLEEP

Why, we must dye it then—

Would I like to stay here indefinitely?
We have trees to prune, cryptograms to decode,
it was all a blind running into the light—
She couldn't say the word for "fish." Nor are his genes undone
by what oafish submarines remain. Aye, sir,
Captain Nemo, sir, we've spotted the junk
in the roads up ahead. What! That spasm I created for my own
    diversion, now
it's clearly emerging out of the octopus drool that so long enshrouded it,
while I, a nether spur to its district railway, am overrun with
coughing doubt for the duration, yet here I must stand,
a seeming enigma. Outside, life prattles on merrily,
like an embroidered towel, and would probably be too weak to object
if we decided to postpone the picnic until November.
I hear you; the arches under the embankment
are part of what I'm all about. I too was weaned from excess
in some silvery age now lost in a blizzard of envelopes.
How frostily jingle the harness bells!
It's all we can do to keep up with the dunce's velocipede,

while in a neutral corner of the quarry
the same binge of history is conning men's eyes
into dogged superstition. So we must make sport of it,
reel in our catch while yet there's time, but droplets
are exploding in the gutter. The gambling ship ferried us away
past larkspur, past concertinas, and the old name became visible again,
briefly, on the building's dusty façade. I

thought we'd lost you. No,
I'm still here.
Do you want to jump out a shy window?
Little by little one took in the foxes' keening:
It's all right, it's sober,

they chortled. This was just a plant,
it counts only for the next time,
and we in beach goggles, brilliant suspenders . . . The party beast
in me says let's abandon, cooler heads say dive,
dive like a frog while famous night is coming on
like the blistered exterior of a sigh.

IN MY HEAD

I walk out over the moors, the hills, the sand valleys.
My head is listless. The wind is scrubbing the stars.
Yet I don't detonate. There is too much land behind me.

Birds sang it once, then not so much anymore.
I am striving to be late, and to kiss a fish.
It would be a greater one who came back
to the ghost frontier.

She wrote on this.

They all taste pretty much the same,
cut flowers, as I was semen in someone's mouth, an avalanche of whorls.
What next for me? Not to be the first one there.

And the wind rattles its scarecrow bones in the living
room, the spring came apart in disorder,
all over the rug. The landsman, he must care,
came too, the others joying his renewal, his removal
as in an old dump truck on the fortieth mile of the road.

Seafaring, the faring, and pickling,
so many admonitions to the Great Lout
who watches over us. He must have approved. In the dimness . . .

Say that this is a street therefore people walk down it.
I stand holding a bunch of keys,
burn up my motto, read Kleist in November.
Can it be that I cannibalize others' lives,
the lives of others' words?
Or am I simply going back to where I came from,
not too long ago, to excuse whoever took my place
when I was gone? Sudden indecision,
dear reddish flowers—I am about a comma in space.
I neither go nor return unfazed.
In short I am this comedy you wrote for me to star in.

Yes she waits, time out, time in,
for me to get the wail, whale of a wail, off my chest.
Yes the coddling circuits
that baited
the time giveaway
are standing all over me too like foxglove angels,
drawing in their breath, giving us what we bargained for—
no crossing, chumps at the end of the market
where needle soldiers ferreted us out,
wished us well, taking a piss at a private hall about
a mile down the road,
coming in during the week.
They had put their kilts on first.
Pull you out of my wool,
toiling as the will
bends us to ends and now is no more.

That force going under,
it kind of makes it stand out
and for me too the trees in this room
we bide our time in, happy as in a nursery,
till the times dictate otherwise. Oh, he was a grown man,
scrofulous it's true, but neither piebald nor land-proud.

A great equator did him in, the fullness of time
waited at the end of my hall, cobbled quodlibets,
procession toward a context. Capitalist
actions forced it into a runoff.
Model villages provide all sorts of
plumbing. Cherry blossoms cascade
in spring, don't last long.
I think we shall be moving to
the dance baths on the river, river that is ripe,
right for explication, as you do plaster it with the wasps
just coming into being, no names yet.
Twenty years ago my dance professor
reinterpreted it, we'll have it on the ground soon
he said coming back, my hand blotted with crystals, your breath calls.
No, something to lug up behind the office at noon.

PROXIMITY

It was great to see you the other day
at the carnival. My enchiladas were delicious,

and I hope that yours were too.
I wanted to fulfill your dream of me

in some suitable way. Giving away my new gloves,
for instance, or putting a box around all that's wrong with us.

But these gutta-percha lamps do not whisper on our behalf.
Now sometimes in the evenings, I am lonely

with dread. A rambunctious wind fills the pine
at my doorstep, the woodbine is enchanted,

and I must be off before the clock strikes
whatever hour it is intent on.

Do not leave me in this wilderness!
Or, if you do, pay me to stay behind.

GOING AWAY ANY TIME SOON

I'll see you in my dreams she said
then they let the gate down
unplugged the coffee
It was time for my annual cure at Wiesbaden

What good are rules anyway
They apply only to themselves and other rules
This rule rules out this other one

The rule of glass, sleek and dark
was poring over my auto-autobiography
like an intensely private person
with hazelnut eyes

When it came time to invent, invest someone or something
you look to the urgent fallen petals
each imbibing its share of life's mystery
as a cat sips and turns away and sips some more

Little mystery are you good for anything?
No she says I came out in time for school
then went back inside to resist sleep
that is still coming as all my absent years are coming

The slower time speaks the less majestic its tower
the fewer bats warbling to interrupt
whatever domestic tasks we believe we have set ourselves
in a truth that is mostly underground

The settled rhythm revives ancient purposes
What did I think going out
and never a tiny random note creeps back in
but all alone a star weeps, watches in the drizzle

and the four magicians fell down.
One took a train to Pennsylvania.

One abstracted his gold hair
picked up a cushion and said

And how is it with you back where you are now?
How many worms to a dozen
How long how many of the others cheat seeing
elbows at this windowsill serious as bunting

on a cloudy day
Which of the antique manners has changed?
For as yet morning is a long way off
Puckered mists trash the hill ecstatic as lozenges

LIKE AMERICA

People are buying store-dolls.
I wonder if that's forbidden too.
Does it mean one isn't to lead one's life?

Today, a day that makes very little sense,
like America,
in clear disarray
everything's getting worse.
Besides, who are we not to endorse it?

And these shattered ornaments to truth
almost grew up to me.
The sun and the yard
paused over a thousand times,
unable to explain the arch that is daylight.

And the tribes that were before
this panicked band announced it was quitting
saw the crocuses too. They were purple and awful.

It's almost leaking to say it.
But how much longer could I go on not missing the point?

Boy I can remember when February
gave out and it was all "no quarter"—the sect of the
levellers passed over and was as night and fire
and more peace. He returned in an hour.
Perpetually flummoxed doorkeepers trying to kill
the men who did the migration proceedings
on the evening news
were backed up all the way to the Arctic Circle.

The aunts were out in zones
of cozy brilliance I
noticed with teapots to their names
like birthing, and they could do Finland then.
It was a kind of parenting. I notice they
doubled our salaries. It was all over
by 6 p.m.

Many causes later he came
in and hurt himself. I
saw a lot of cherry bombs. Is this the place
where one foregathers?
If so, what are all the urchins doing?
Oh she warned it's just to the end of the block
where knee-high tulips pucker and all is reassuring
as they'd rather not have you believe. Does
that clear everything up? Well I think so well I
would like to see the proof of the invitation:
a hand print. I'm so sorry these are inexcusable.
I'll dust myself up, or off;
meanwhile in the clearing they are pouring something.
Do you think you could be kind to come in

and matter where the horse esteems mechanized shortcuts?
Say rather he came in and hurt himself,
and now the bagpipers have nothing left to mourn,

the day just wheezes and goes down a funnel
counterclockwise. It was all just a fit
to have made you start bolt upright
on the steppe terns parted from
with little glovelike cries
awaiting the refrigerator that was to have us all
on its digital menu.
Wait, there are extenuating circumstances
and I myself am just a bum;
whatever came in with the weather
and dematerialized in the corners of the room, just so
am I to myself and others around.
But how do you justify

the crank silhouetted against the sky?
That's just it, I don't; it is all leftovers
and why am I crying
when the boats pass
in the narrow ship channel
with corduroy undies for all the years
I took off from Mrs. Bacon's
and the way they came flooding back at me
like complaints in a gyroscope
or an armillary of vexations.
Then she proposed take this needle
and thread it for the two
messages you have missed.

I'll not start another reptile war;
I look to the end of the komodo dragons thundering overhead.
Otherwise I sleep under the eaves; the cabbages
keep me company at evening, and are all
the society anyone wants. And Yes,
I keep up the sewing, the round robin
of Lettergate wherever a spare postal employer

taxes us with unlived puns: *There*
do we stop and pitch camp,
and I'll tell you it's not going to get easier,
only harder.
With that they

took off, just a bundle
of stems to make a totem with.
I sit on the site over and over,
let it absorb hard doing,
piecemeal reconciliations, laundry
marks rubbed out in the wash, seasonal
hares and conviviality and the rest,
the rest.

WHITEOUT

More and more obviously, the trainer won't handle things
his way, or ours—beats me how cute everything *used* to be.
We stood poised in a circle, and
some note of admiration bloomed and faded.
The cow was coming to ask our forgiveness
for the blue flax. Then everybody segued into a canon,
more ships were lost, more men at sea, the carload of opals
bringing bad luck from Anatolia. And in a wash,
it was gone. No more having to pick up one's room,
one's socks.

Luckily there is an umpire who sees that
behavior is coded, that it all shakes down into the mesh
where the train never minded, that there is still fun out on the horizon.
The blues—did we mention that?
And the energy that was coming to unsex all but the lifeless on Mars,
the initiated, grasping at handlebars.

A FRENCH STAMP

Of handedness and the Brothers Handedness,
too often that tale had been told by Yore,
fifth-century scribe. He liked inking in details.

If one is a cigarette lighter
that's lonely, which is lonely. Or a tricycle
coasting in gales, there is a secret satisfaction

fins emulate. Here, keep my scalp,
I'm seeing a pattern here, divestiture of some knave.
It was likely to be our last onus, this plaid scarecrow
out of a Braille encyclopedia. Hurry with the milk,
be here. Fortune placed tots in escrow. Good to monitor 'em,

go with the feed. In Manhattan merely
two minutes to two, moonlit torso returns. Sheesh.
Some abbey's got him. Let Fido lick
last year's olive branch. I'm outta here.
I told you, no way, it's dorsal.

ONE MAN'S POEM

John came into town at night
and the clock was striking.
The damn boat leaked. Well, I . . .
It *was* pretty unusual.

Never mind, hand me that eyesore.
He came to see a tailor.
More about it I do not know
out on the canal.

The twins schlepped raisins and plums,
my dogbeat, for as far as we forgotten
come together to make sense
by midnight's shattered drum.

There was more walking around and talking.
Then all got into a car and drove away.
Its tail was silver red, and a
banjo stood on end in the car.

The waves of freshman and sophomore grief
slide by me somehow.
We are old and dated
and cannot of our lives make any sense.

It was in the way he put it to me,
muddied or on a rock
at the center of a field puts us to shame.
There is more than the spirit jabs,

under the little hollow birds creep
and are asked forgiveness. Some are afraid
that they will fly away.
By morning all is shot to hell.

THE PATHETIC FALLACY

A cautionary mister,
the thaumaturge poked holes in my trope.
I said what are you doing that for.
His theorem wasn't too complicated,

just complicated enough. In brief,
this was it. The governor should peel
no more shadow apples, and about teatime
it was as if the lemon of Descartes
had risen to full prominence on the opulent skyline.

There were children in drawers, and others trying to shovel them out.
In a word, shopping had never been so tenuous,

but it seems *we* had let the cat out of the bag, in spurts.
Often, from that balcony
I'd interrogate the jutting profile of night
for what few psalms or coins it might
in other circumstances have been tempted to shower down
on the feeble heathen oppressor, and my wife.

Always you get the same bedizened answer back.
It was like something else, or it wasn't,
and if it wasn't going to be as much, why,
it might as well be less, for all anyone'd care.
And the ditches brought it home dramatically
to the horizon, socked the airport in.

We, we are only mad clouds,
a dauphin's reach from civilization,
with its perfumed citadels, its quotas. What did that
mean you were going to do to *me*?
Why, in another land and time we'd be situated, separate
from each other and the ooze of life. But here, within

the palisade of brambles it only comes often enough to what
can be sloughed off quickly, with the least amount of fuss.
For the ebony cage claims its constituents

as all were going away, thankful the affair had ended.

As rain cobbles itself
    together, puts an expectant face
on things, we lived those
greasy times. Sordid
with excess rapture, blue
as a cow's face. We came out of it pretty well
    at the end.

Worth looking up, these tepid old
    things

could still jiggle
a thug's arms, thrum the upholstery's
lilacs. Warehouses make like
marauding castles in the heat, I am always steep
when being remembered.
                      Ash on a coed's face,
this barren step planted in Thieves' Row, more where
your mother muddled all things. And if it be not,
where is its funnel—pass the luster,
please, something's abiding: love-in-a-storm,
it says.

MANY COLORS

There is a chastening to it,
a hymnlike hemline.
Hyperbole in another disguise.

Dainty foresters walk through it.

On the splashed polyester walls
a tooth fairy held court. And that was like mud gravy,
a sop to the reigning *idées reçues.*
It's all too—
charming.
It makes you want to scream
and hug your neighbor like he was your best friend.

I'm over my head with it.
Suddenly there was a travelling salesman with balls,
like an ant on V-J day.

And easing through the night we felt scoops
of clay like tired ice cream.
Here, here's your vigil. Now get it out of here. One of us—
Gus the plumber—is entranced.

Of course you could let them come to you
as if you'd asked, and don't blame it on me
when they get silted up to the snow line.
A master craftsman is coming to stay with you, to save you.

Yes and my horse knew all about this
but wasn't letting on
until the time you and I got over the fix on his importance he had,
only to discover another's hip-huggers in the brown dust
under the mailbox.

And we all came quietly.

In what axis I've heard you ringing—
there is no time to do that.
This is no time to do that.
The passion police are on your case
and we'll get back to picking winners anon, at eventide,
asunder.

Go blow. Tremble. Decipher. Mix and match.
Maybe. We'll see.

AUTUMN IN THE LONG AVENUE

I see and hear the wind.
It is unreceived. Clouds flee backwards.
I think myself into a stupor.

Once upon a time everybody was here.
Then the pellets started to go.
They move and move little,
like my brother or childhood,
or a little schoolhouse
near the zoo, boarded up with directions
to some other telltale structure, crusted
with scaffolding like frosting on winter's cake,
to tell you, go through, go through now,
die and formally die.

Yet autumn stays sequestered
and likes it. In that period
some people still came to visit, with nothing
on their minds, no reason, not even liking you.
A lot of autos stormed the site
of the one pine's expiration, breathing, asking
for you. Some said you had gone,
but you were hiding under the porch, stung
with remorse. Now this person
comes and says have you seen the shed,
it gives me goose bumps, and I, stuck as always on
which word should be the first, but comes out
in no particular order, volunteer my notes on the
time we sat with woodpeckers on the
various counterpane and had a swig—
when you were, I mean, on the fence,
just inside, talking the way people in dreams
talk to those who are awake, subverting the last
ditch of defense in time for what
takes it away . . .

The light of late afternoon
chiseled the sea and barracks, but who
was keeping count? There were more tourists
than usual that day, the town seemed to run away from them
as we approached them, wondering what was wrong, what was the matter
with the bland corpses they had come to see name
something we ourselves couldn't see for being in it
as mute pedestrians moved to adjourn it.
I've seen it before, I've seen it in the street:
These various resolutions fade in and out,
plaiting a track on the texture of day,
a legacy of distant effort, wispy
and traditional, like dads and moms coming off
the assembly line. But they never get that right.
I just said goodbye.

SNOW

As a fish spoils
in a time of truce, so these galoshes go
hopping over sidewalk and snowbank, not really knowing
to whose destiny we are being summoned
or what happens after that.

As time spoils,
it may have known what it was doing
but decided not to do anything about it, so everything is lost,
wrapped in a landfill. It could be caviar
or the New York *Daily News*.

After all, *I* come next,
he said, am a cruel object like all the torsos
you unbuttoned all over your previous life, scant in comparison
to this one, and I said, go ahead and quit clowning
if you like that game, but

leave me beside myself,
like a kid next to a lamppost. Okay, what gain
in not replying? What capitalist system do you think this is? Surely
it's late capitalism, by which I mean not to go
yet and peace undermines

the uproar we all made
about it, and you are positively put on hold
again. I like the mouse in this turmoil, not exactly purring
adroitly, not seeming to conjugate the
avalanche of fear.

Now when Norsemen
(or some substitute) tumble out of the north, sifting
down over our busy, shuttered, dignified street with hints of the Azores,
there's no untangling the knots we put there before
and paused to identify

as the four winds rushed
in and purified the place of partnerships,
fanning overhead, a-bristle with doodads, chafing at every chime
from every earnest steeple, coughing too much.
The little guy was

impatient, was serious,
every time a blow fell adjured another conspirator,
and so, when it got quite dark we became an outing, another
quilting-bee disaster. And if it tried too far
there was always salt to rub

in wounds to be licked.

WITHIN THE HOUR

The tea is too hot.
The curtain in the window blew around.
Rind rotting on brown chairs.
In the valley of bartenders the one-eyed stooge is king.

What I'm doing now is write.
That's the real stuff.
It doesn't work!
I got a card from him yesterday I could ask Dick.

What is the fresh approach?
Your mini body coming unto me, unshelled
as peace pavanes no one undertakes,
not without a woofing in the chest-o-ciser,

two strokes and it's gone.
You owed the fresh kind.
Why yes. Remember
me? Remember me
in any case.

THE DONG WITH THE LUMINOUS NOSE
(a cento)

Within a windowed niche of that high hall
I wake and feel the fell of dark, not day.
I shall rush out as I am, and walk the street
Hard by yon wood, now smiling as in scorn.
The lights begin to twinkle from the rocks
From camp to camp, through the foul womb of night.
Come, Shepherd, and again renew the quest.
And birds sit brooding in the snow.

Continuous as the stars that shine,
When all men were asleep the snow came flying
Near where the dirty Thames does flow
Through caverns measureless to man,
Where thou shalt see the red-gilled fishes leap
And a lovely Monkey with lollipop paws
Where the remote Bermudas ride.

Softly, in the dusk, a woman is singing to me:
This is the cock that crowed in the morn.
Who'll be the parson?
Beppo! That beard of yours becomes you not!
A gentle answer did the old Man make:
Farewell, ungrateful traitor,
Bright as a seedsman's packet
Where the quiet-coloured end of evening smiles.

Obscurest night involved the sky
And brickdust Moll had screamed through half a street:
"Look in my face; my name is Might-have-been,
Sylvan historian, who canst thus express
Every night and alle,
The happy highways where I went
To the hills of Chankly Bore!"

Where are you going to, my pretty maid?
These lovers fled away into the storm
And it's O dear, what can the matter be?
For the wind is in the palm-trees, and the temple bells they say:
Lay your sleeping head, my love,
On the wide level of a mountain's head,
Thoughtless as monarch oaks, that shade the plain,
In autumn, on the skirts of Bagley Wood.
A ship is floating in the harbour now,
Heavy as frost, and deep almost as life!

COME ON, DEAR

It was another era, almost another century,
I was going to say. The saint wept quietly
in her ebony pew. It was the thing to do.
Then garlands of laughter, studded with cloves and lemons,
joined the standing figures with their distant nimbi.
Inexplicably, all was well for a time.

Soon, discordant echoes reined in the heyday:
It was love, after all,
that everybody was talking about
and nobody gave a shit for.
But why am I telling *you* about all this, who wrote the book,
who stamped his initials in the fairway
for all blokes to see? And if it only came
down to this smidgen, would apes and penguins be any wiser
for all the tunnels of love we shuffled through,
scared by skeletons, by bats, at every turning
of our loose-leafed trajectory through shallow water?

Only when the iodine sunset
bleeds again against red day, will all children
get permission to go out where the grass is short,
where the absent-minded postman leaves earnests of his passing
from this day to the next, where the eaves are clipped
close to the houses. Five days from the last clerestory
your ambiance drained into the pockmarked shutters.
Obviously the jig was up. What's that? Whose jig? O I can see clear
ahead into the flying; the poor don't talk much about it,
but her apron is ambrosial with trellised stars,
her stance stares down even the most unquiet,
and on days like this you ride free.
There was such numismatics in his pocket
as only jitterbugs in cyberspace could conjugate
while from fate's awning the diamond drip descended, bigger
than both of us, big as all outdoors.

GENTLE READER

Abruptly, unassertively, the year starts,
as freeways close and roofs collapse,
and all kinds of incidents give nervure to the map:
a stitch in time, a local hero here,
boys falling in tune with the ageless argument.

So out of the turquoise turmoil a name
implodes like a star, having made its point.
And the seasons, welcome as you know,
are seen packing it in. Maybe add some rust
at a crucial jointure, no? But who am I
to be telling you your business. Next, young and beautiful,
emerging from a door, casting your essence
along the face of today's precipice, you see "there's no tomorrow,"
only avatars waiting in the wings, more or less patiently.
This is what it takes for you to do what's best,
covering all the exits.

Oh, there is a danger there?
Who would have thought it in today's heat?
But on the other hand, why just be standing
while its morose page rolls over,
an encumbrance to all, not just ourselves?
And when twilight licks appreciatively at the sky,
your answer will be there in the circuitry,
not bypassed. For you to hold,
to genuflect with.

A shadow of a flagon crossed your face:
The cease-fire is improving?
And in this starting to be in something, what had the older
children been doing? Taking lessons still to be paid for,
impinging on what comes next. Comes now.

Soon there is something to be said for everything,
he said, whiplash, whippets; why even my identity
is strange to me now, a curiosity. When someone comes later,
who will I be talking with? The erroneous vision
made no mention of this. Its conquering agenda is complete,
and we, of course, are incomplete, destined to ourselves
and its fitful version of eternity:
the one with chapter titles.
More worldliness to celebrate. And yet, someone
will take it from you, needy thing.

HOMECOMING

Weather drips quietly through the skeins
in my diary. What surly elision is this?

Who faxed the folks news of my homecoming,
even unto the platform number? The majestic parlor car
slides neatly into its berth, the doors fly open,
and it's Jean and Marcy and all the kids, waving pink plastic pinwheels,
chomping on popcorn. Ngarrrh. You know I adore ceremony,
even while refusing to stand on it, but this, this is too inane.
And the cold anonymity of the station takes over,
reins in the crowds that were sifting to the furthest exits. No one is here.
Now I know why I've always hated the tango, yet loved the intimacy
secreted in its curls. And for this to continue, we've got to
get together, renew old saws, let old grudges ride . . .

Later I'm posting this to you.
I just thought of you, you see, as indeed I do
several million times a day. I need your disapproval,
can't live without your churlish ways.

DATE DUE